I SEE ANIMAL TEXT

FEATHERS

by Jenna Lee Gleisner

TABLE OF CONTENTS

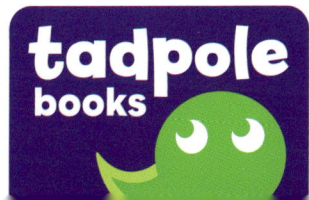

tadpole books

WORDS TO KNOW

blue

feathers

fluffy

red

spotted

striped

FEATHERS

feather

I see feathers.

I see red feathers.

I see blue feathers.

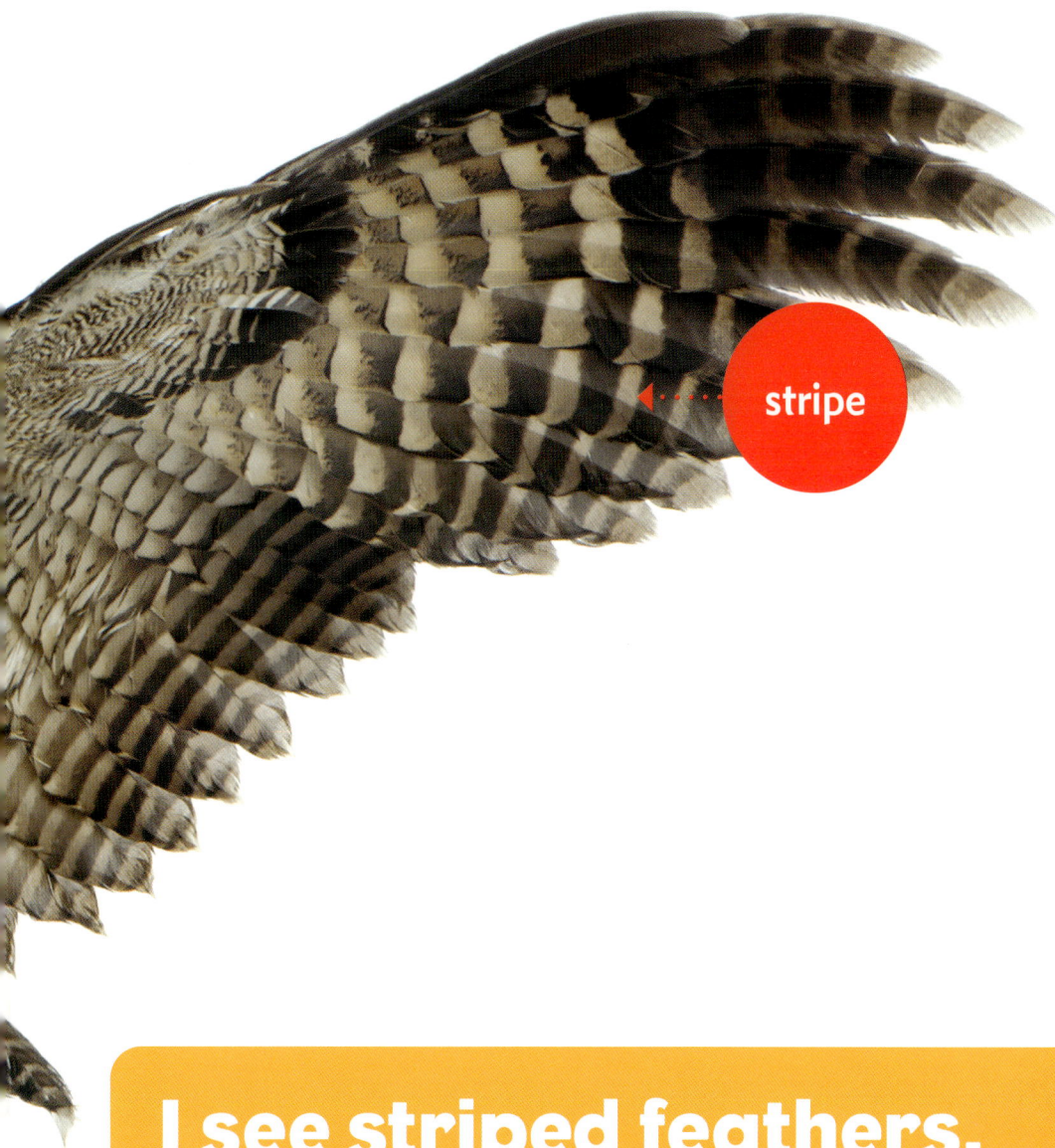

stripe

I see striped feathers.

spot

I see tall feathers!

15

LET'S REVIEW!

Feathers help birds fly. They also help birds blend in, show off, and keep warm. What kinds of feathers do you see below?

INDEX

16